Old TOLLCROSS, MORNINGSIDE and SWANS

by

Malcolm Cant

This photograph, with the Roarin' Shepherd's Cottage on the left, is typical of Swanston during the first decade of the twentieth century. The shepherd in question was John Todd, who became a close friend of Robert Louis Stevenson when the latter spent the summer months at Swanston Cottage.

ISBN 9781840331707

THE PUBLISHERS REGRET THAT THEY CANNOT SUPPLY
COPIES OF ANY PICTURES FEATURED IN THIS BOOK.

ACKNOWLEDGEMENTS

The publishers would like to thank Mrs Louise Jenkins for allowing the use
of images from her collection of Morningside postcards in this book.

FURTHER READING

The books listed below were used by the author during his research.
None of them are available from Stenlake Publishing. Those interested in
finding out more are advised to contact their local bookshop or reference
library.

Dunlop, A. Ian, *The Kirks of Edinburgh*, 1988
Gifford, McWilliam & Walker, *The Buildings of Scotland – Edinburgh*, 1984
Harris, Stuart, *The Place Names of Edinburgh*, 1996
Hunter, D. L. G., *Edinburgh's Transport*, 1964
Hunter, D. L. G., *Edinburgh's Transport: The Corporation Years*, 1999
Mullay, Sandy, *The Edinburgh Encyclopedia*, 1996
Smith, Charles J., *Historic South Edinburgh*, 2001

2. Craiglea Drive, Morningside, Edinburgh

Craiglea Drive, looking west towards
Morningside Grove, near the junction
with St Fillan's Terrace. The drive was
built around 1884 with the side streets
of Dalhousie Terrace, St Ronan's Terrace
and St Fillan's Terrace begun a few years
later.

INTRODUCTION

There are many places of historical interest along the comparatively short journey between Tollcross and Swanston. The arterial road from the Old Town of Edinburgh now passes through several busy suburbs, many of which are not even mentioned on early nineteenth-century maps of the city. On the other hand the basic layout of the main roads and some of the places of interest are still clearly identifiable. *Kirkwood's Plan of Edinburgh* (1817) shows the old road, Cowfeeder Row (later called High Riggs) leading southwards from Main Point, at the junction of West Port, High Riggs and Bread Street, to meet Lothian Road at Tollcross. Tempting as it is to speculate about the derivation of the name Tollcross, there is, in fact, no evidence that there was ever a toll there. The nearest toll was at Wrightshouses a few hundred yards to the south.

The old Linton or Biggar road ran south from Tollcross through the district of Bruntsfield, which was originally laid out with substantial detached villas where the tenement buildings now stand. The larger properties were Greenhill House on the east side of the road, and farther south, Falcon Hall near present-day Falcon Avenue. The village of Morningside consisted of the parish church, the village school, rows of modest cottages and one or two larger properties standing in their own grounds. Briggs of Braid was on the south-east side of the small bridge which carried the main road over the Jordan Burn near the present-day post office in Morningside Road. Morningside Toll stood here from the 1850s until 1883 when it was dismantled and re-erected as a lodge house at the entrance to the Hermitage of Braid. About 1830 a substantial alteration was made to the alignment of the turnpike road south of

what was later the position of Morningside Road Station. In order to avoid several steep gradients and awkward corners on Braid Road, especially in the winter, a new section of road was built to the west along the line of what is now Comiston Road and Pentland Terrace, merging again with the old Braid Road at Buckstone. Prior to the construction of this new section of roadway, the fields of Greenbank Farm stretched from about the position of the former City Hospital eastwards to the old Braid Road to include areas such as Riselaw.

Of all the locations covered by this selection of photographs, perhaps the village of Swanston has survived most intact, though only after a period of severe decline in the 1950s. Its idyllic position, with thatched cottages nestling at the base of the Pentland Hills, and its connection with Robert Louis Stevenson, ensure that Swanston will remain one of Edinburgh's most romantic settings for many years to come.

Malcolm Cant, June 2001

Right: Springvalley Terrace made an ideal playground for local children in 1915. It took its name from Springvalley House, demolished in 1907, the site of which is commemorated in a stone plaque on the face of the tenement at the north-west end of the terrace. For many years Springvalley House was the home of James Grant, author of *Old & New Edinburgh.*

The Central Hall in Earl Grey Street has been the home of the Methodist Church since the building, designed by the architects Dunn & Findlay, was erected in 1901. The entrance in Thornybauk, flanked by Ionic pillars, opens directly onto a flight of stairs leading to the hall above, which has a curved and ribbed ceiling. Most of the ground floor facing Earl Grey Street was constructed as retail units, their rents helping to defray the cost of erecting the building. Earl Grey Street was laid out in 1785 as part of Lothian Road. It became Wellington Street around 1824 and Earl Grey Street in 1832. The entire east side was demolished in the 1970s but failed to attract further development (despite many abortive attempts) until 2000, when the Bank of Scotland built stylish new offices and shops along its whole length. Fleming's Stores sold a variety of ironmongery and hardware, while on the right-hand side of the picture, the shop with the mortar and pestle outside was for many years occupied by the Scottish Drug Co. Ltd.

This picture of the Tollcross junction probably dates from the late 1920s or early 1930s. The model horse, belonging to the Royal Riding Academy and discernible in the picture on the front cover, has gone from the wallhead of 16 Home Street, and the electric tram system with its overhead power lines has replaced the old cable-driven system. Small islands in the middle of the roadway for people to queue on were a feature of the electric tram system in the city centre: one such island can be seen on the right of the picture. Passengers wanting to travel south towards Morningside queued on the larger triangular-shaped island to the left. This island was also home to the famous Tollcross clock and an underground gents' toilet.

This classic photograph, taken at the corner of Tarvit Street and Leven Street, conveys the full character of the area before the construction of the King's Theatre on the site in 1906. The corner premises were occupied by a branch of Covent Garden Leith, selling strawberries, gooseberries and cut flowers. No. 2 Leven Street (below the advertisement for Thomson's Oatmeal) is occupied by T. J. Malcolmson, grocer & wine merchant, and No. 4 by a gilder and restorer of paintings. The tall chimney belonged to the Drumdryan Brewery, which was founded in 1760 and demolished in 1904. It would have been demolished much earlier had plans to bring a branch of the Union Canal through Tollcross been implemented. In 1813, Hugh Baird proposed that the branch be cut through Gilmore Place and across the Meadows, but the idea was abandoned on the grounds of cost. The overall cost of the Union Canal, estimated at £235,167, was already over-budget.

KING'S THEATRE

KINGS THEATRE, EDINBURGH

The King's Theatre was built in red sandstone by W. S. Cruikshank & Sons of Lower Gilmore Place to designs by the architects J. D. Swanston and James Davidson. The foundation stone was laid on 18 August 1906 by Andrew Carnegie, the Scots-born millionaire who made his fortune in the American steel industry. The opening performance, on 8 December 1906, was of the pantomime *Cinderella*. For many years the King's was owned by the Cruikshank family, who continued as managers after the theatre was acquired by Howard & Wyndham. The canopy, seen in the picture over the main entrance, was removed many years ago, and internally the upper (of three) galleries, affectionately known by Edinburgh theatre-goers as 'the Gods', was also removed and the interior remodelled. Over the years the King's has attracted stars of the highest quality in pantomimes, musicals, comedy, drama and opera. Among the many film stars to appear in earlier years were Katharine Hepburn, Jack Hawkins and Stewart Grainger.

Gillespie's Hospital in Gillespie Crescent, designed in 1801 by the architect William Burn, was built on the site of a fourteenth-century mansion, Wrychtishousis, which was demolished to make way for the new building. The money to establish 'a Hospital for aged men and women and a Free School for boys', to be managed by the Edinburgh Merchant Company as trustees, was provided from the estate of James Gillespie of Spylaw. Gillespie, born in 1726, lived at Spylaw House, at the rear of which was Spylaw Mill on the Water of Leith in which he manufactured snuff. With the assistance of his brother John, who ran the retail shop in the High Street, he built up a very successful business in the snuff trade. When James died in 1797 he left the greater part of his estate to build the hospital and school. The former was opened in 1802 and the following year the first Gillespie's School for boys was built in Bruntsfield Place. In 1908 the administration of the school was transferred to the Edinburgh School Board, and in 1922 the hospital building in Gillespie Crescent (above) was acquired by the Royal Blind Asylum who remained there until the mid-1970s. Unfortunately, not only did the city lose Wrychtishousis in 1801 but also Gillespie's Hospital, when the building was demolished and replaced by a block of flats designed by Ian H. Rolland Associates in 1976.

Bruntsfield Place and Links, Edinburgh

Bruntsfield Links, the last remnant of the once-famous Burgh Muir, was at one time a popular hunting ground of the Scottish nobility. It was greatly reduced in size when land was feued around Tarvit Street and Greenhill, but has been protected against further encroachment by the Edinburgh Improvement Act of 1827. As early as the sixteenth century there are references to 'the great stone quarries near the lands of Brownfield' (Bruntsfield), some of which were still in existence when the Marchmont tenements were being built at the end of the nineteenth century. Golf has been played on the links almost from time immemorial. Several important clubs were established there, the most ancient being the Burgess Golf Society, founded in 1735, forerunner of the Royal Burgess Golfing Society of Edinburgh. Another of the early clubs was the Bruntsfield, founded in 1761, now the Bruntsfield Links Golfing Society at Barnton. The photograph shows Bruntsfield Place with the Bruntsfield Hotel to the left of the tree in the centre. The spire belongs to Bruntsfield Evangelical Church (formerly Church of Scotland) in Leamington Terrace. The building dates from 1882 and was designed by J. Russell Walker.

Boroughmuir School was designed in 1911 by John A. Carfrae, architect to the Edinburgh School Board, and opened on 19 January 1914 by T. McKinnon Wood, then described as the Secretary for Scotland. This aerial view gives a good idea of the basic plan of the building, which has two large light-wells each containing a gymnasium at basement level. Boroughmuir was established in 1904 in a new building erected in Warrender Park Crescent, but this was quickly found to be too small and the school was moved to Viewforth. For many years the former building was used by James Gillespie's High School for Girls, but in 1972 Boroughmuir took it over again as their junior school. In 1990, following a major programme of upgrading at Viewforth, all classes were again brought under the same roof. A short ceremony held to mark the occasion was attended by a large group of present and past pupils and teachers, including R. L. S. Carswell, headmaster from 1946 to 1967, L. L. Romanis, headmaster from 1967 to 1982, and the then headteacher, T. W. Dalgleish.

Bruntsfield Place looking south near the junction with Viewforth. Prior to about 1880, Bruntsfield Place was lined on the west side (right-hand side of the picture) with large detached villas which were demolished to make way for the tenements seen here. These were designed by Edward Calvert and Dunn & Findlay. Most Edinburgh tenements are four storeys in height, but on either side of Bruntsfield Place they have four full storeys above the shops at ground level. The very grand tenement houses on the left of the picture were built in the 1880s to designs by the architect George Washington Browne, who also designed the Royal Sick Children's Hospital in Sciennes Road. Browne's tenements were built on the estate of the old mansion of Greenhill House, which stood between present-day Bruntsfield Place and Forbes Road. The shop on the near corner of Viewforth is P. R. Beattie, chemist and druggist, while on the extreme right of the picture is a branch of the Maypole Dairy Co.

Bruntsfield Primary School, in Montpelier, was provisionally designed by the Edinburgh School Board architect Robert Wilson and completed by his successor, John A. Carfrae, in 1893. This view of the symmetrical frontage, taken from Bruntsfield Avenue, clearly shows the central windows of the two halls (one above the other) flanked by two 'wings', both of which incorporate the School Board roundel between the first and second floors.

Blanche & Co., Wine & Italian Warehousemen, were established at 31 South Bruntsfield Place around 1888. At that time other family members had similar shops at St Leonard's Street, Nicolson Street and Dalkeith Road. Around 1890 the shop address was changed by the General Post Office from 31 South Bruntsfield Place to 155 Bruntsfield Place, and the firm gradually expanded to include Nos. 155, 157 and 159. This picture shows Blanche's delivery carts in Bruntsfield Gardens with Bruntsfield Place in the background. After the company ceased trading around 1970 the premises were occupied for many years by Nastiuks and then by Peckhams.

BLANCHE & CO.,
155 and 157 BRUNTSFIELD PLACE, EDINBURGH.

Barclay Church was completed in 1864, primarily with a legacy of £10,000 left by Miss Mary Barclay, who had been a member of Free Tolbooth Church. Its ornate 250-foot spire, supported by massive, corbelled stonework, is unmistakably the work of the architect Frederick T. Pilkington, whose design was selected from those of six competing architects. The nave has two galleries, one above the other, and a central pulpit behind which are the organ pipes. The church was built with an entrance hall and church officer's house, but the larger hall to the east, designed by Sydney Mitchell & Wilson, was not added until 1891. It was initially called Barclay Free Church and after numerous variations in the name became Barclay Church in 1980. Glengyle Terrace, with the young trees hardly obscuring the view over Bruntsfield Links, was built in the late 1860s by W. & D. McGregor to designs by the architect David MacGibbon.

The buildings in Bruntsfield Place and Barclay Terrace have hardly changed in the last hundred years, but the shopfronts and modes of transport have altered completely. Other than the cable car, all transport is horse-drawn from heavy working carts to more refined, covered carriages with the coachman perched at the front. The shop on the corner of Bruntsfield Place and Barclay Terrace is, appropriately, a coach office, and No. 2 Barclay Terrace (behind the pavement drinking well) is Miss J. Butler's registry for servants. On the left of the picture a sign advertises Thomson's Dye Works in Perth, while further down the street at 35 & 37 Bruntsfield Place is E. J. Stechan, the picture frame maker.

This photograph was probably taken in the 1920s, quite a bit after the 'golden age' of picture postcards. The overhead electric cables for the tram system would not have been introduced until after 1923. The row of shops on the right-hand side of the picture includes some well-known names of the day. Farthest from the camera, with the large white blind, is Hughes, the fishmonger (still trading), then (nearer to the camera) the British Linen Bank and the Cereal Produce Co. On the extreme right is the coal office operated by Bruce Lindsay Bros. Other traders who operated in this section at various dates in the 1920s were: Mdme. Robert, costumier; A. Sinclair, tobacconist; and Duncan Munro, tailor and clothier. To the right of the lady carrying the youngster is a sign reading 'CARS TO TOWN STOP HERE', referring, of course, to the electric car system. The tenement buildings, numbering four storeys above the shops, were the work of Hippolyte Blanc, who also designed Christ Church Episcopal nearby.

Morningside Road & Christchurch, Edinburgh   340/364

Looking north from Holy Corner towards Boroughmuirhead. The steeple belongs to Christ Church Episcopal, designed in the French-Gothic style by the architect Hippolyte J. Blanc, who was also a member of the congregation. The builders were W. & J. Kirkwood, who had finished only part of the work by the time the church was opened on 4 June 1876. Construction of the chancel, tower and spire was completed later by a gift from Miss Falconar of Falcon Hall in Morningside Road, given in memory of her father, a founder member of Morningside Parish Church. The substantial two-storey building with dormer windows to the left was designed in 1873 by Peddie & Kinnear as a branch office for the Bank of Scotland.

16

Morningside Road looking north to Holy Corner, with the spire of Christ Church Episcopal on the left and the square tower of what is now the Eric Liddell Centre to the right. Three interesting shop signs protrude from the front of the tenement on the left: first, the mortar and pestle of James Kirk, chemist; second, a fish denoting the presence of G. Campbell & Son, fishmongers; and third, a branch office sign for *The Scotsman* and *Dispatch* newspapers which dealt with local entries for births, deaths and marriages, among other things. The open-topped cable car carries the destination board 'Braid Hills Road'. In wet weather passengers on the top deck had very little protection from the weather. However, at least they could keep their knees reasonably dry by using the small canvas shield which could be drawn out from the back of the seat in front.

A busy scene at the junction of Morningside Road and Church Hill with open-topped cable car No. 103 travelling south towards Morningside Station. The premises on the right corner are occupied by the Clydesdale Bank, adjacent to which is Thomas Piper's cycle shop. On the opposite pavement, at No. 66, James Rose the family grocer has a prominent sign on the gable wall of his shopfront. The striped blind is at Dobson's the butcher, to the left of which is Colquhoun, the confectioner.

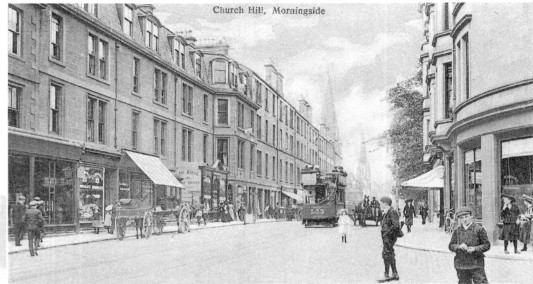

Church Hill, Morningside

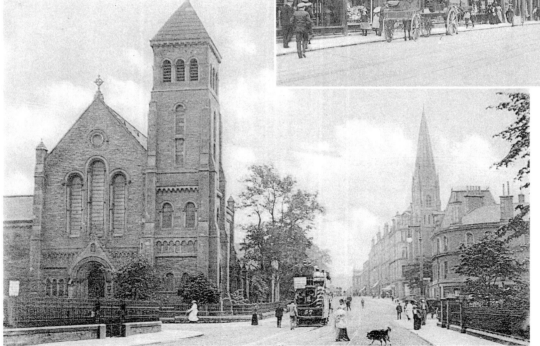

Morningside Road looking south towards Church Hill, with the former North Morningside United Presbyterian Church, dating from 1881, on the left. In 1980 North Morningside and Morningside Congregational Churches joined forces to form Morningside United Church, located on the north side of Chamberlain Road. The vacated building (illustrated here) then became the Eric Liddell Centre, named after the Olympic runner and missionary known to the world through the film *Chariots of Fire*, who was a member of Morningside Congregational Church. The church on the right of the picture was designed in 1872 by MacGibbon & Ross for the Free Church. When its congregation moved to a new building (now the Church Hill Theatre) in 1894, the old building became Morningside Baptist Church. Following a serious fire in 1973 this was remodelled internally by David Carr, architects.

Morningside Parish Church, on the north corner of Morningside Road and Newbattle Terrace, was opened on 29 July 1838 following a very successful appeal for funds during the previous year. A long list of subscribers, headed by Alexander Falconar of Falcon Hall and his five daughters, pledged over £2,000, well in excess of the estimated cost of £1,600. Architect John Henderson provided plans for 634 sittings, and the plot of land was gifted by Sir John Stuart Forbes, proprietor of the lands of Greenhill. The church bell came from Whitechapel Foundry and in 1840 the congregation bought the mechanism of the clock from the Old Schoolhouse across the road. This remained in the church until 1929 when it was replaced for £64. In 1990 Morningside Parish Church was closed for worship when its congregation amalgamated with that of Braid Church. The redundant building was sold to Napier University, and Braid Church became the home of the combined congregation under the name Morningside Braid Parish Church.

One of the most significant buildings to survive from the old village of Morningside is the Old Schoolhouse, dating from 1823. It lies on the west side of Morningside Road to the north of Cuddy Lane. Four eminent citizens were closely involved in its formation: George Ross of Woodburn House; Alexander Falconar of Falcon Hall; James Evans of Canaan Park; and Henry Hare of Newgrange. It was George Ross, the distinguished judge, whose interest and financial backing ensured the continuation of the school, which became known as the Ross School. After the Old Schoolhouse closed, the building was let in 1906 to the Christian Brethren as a place of worship. They subsequently bought it, extended it by the addition of small wings to the north and south, and overhauled the clock. Unlike the former parish church, this building is still in use as a place of worship.

In the 1820s Alexander Falconar built Falcon Hall on the Canaan estate, on the east side of Morningside Road, possibly incorporating an earlier house known as Morningside Lodge. Designed by the architect Thomas Hamilton, it was a grand building of two principal storeys with a facade of twelve monolithic pillars. Four of these created an imposing entrance, above which eight more supported a broad pediment. On the ground floor the pillars were flanked by statues of Nelson and Wellington, while stone falcons stood alongside the upper ones. After the last of the five Falconar daughters died in 1887, the hall became a boarding school for boys called Morningside College. The last person to occupy the building as a home was John George Bartholomew. When he moved out in 1907 to allow redevelopment of the site, he undertook the huge task of dismantling and rebuilding the hall's central facade, which was incorporated in the front of his new premises, the Edinburgh Geographical Institute in Duncan Street, where it can still be seen today. The hall's gates and pillars, also incorporating falcons, now stand at the entrance to Edinburgh Zoo.

Morningside Road looking south near the junction with Falcon Road West around 1912. The double pedimented roofline of Morningside Public Library can be seen on the right. The library was opened on 9 November 1904 by John Harrison, the second son of Lord Provost George Harrison, on a site previously occupied by Denholm's Smiddy. Nearer to the camera, the gap between the two buildings was occupied by David Davidson & Son, monumental sculptors, with the Blackford Press in the adjacent building. Both the sculptor's yard and the printing works were demolished for the construction of the Merlin Lounge Bar. The tenements on the left-hand side of the road replaced a row of small cottages which backed onto the grounds of Falcon Hall.

Looking up Morningside Road from the junction with Maxwell Street around 1906, when the district was served by open-topped cable cars. The large premises on the corner of Maxwell Street are occupied by the South Morningside branch of the Union Bank of Scotland Ltd. Other shops in the section from the bank (No. 372) going towards Millar Crescent are: Richard Leishman, dairy (No. 370); Margaret Henderson Burn, draper (No. 366); John G. Shand & Co., house painters (No. 364); and Alexander McGregor, hairdresser and perfumer (No. 360). The high railings beside the pavement on the other side of the road enclosed a small plantation of trees which at one time belonged to the owners of the houses in Hermitage Terrace.

Morningside Road looking North, Edinburgh.

Morningside Road looking north *c*.1909, with Millar Crescent on the left and Jordan Lane on the right. The two-storey building in the foreground is occupied at street level by R. M. Millar, house agent and valuer. At the rear of this building, the Brotherston family ran the Morningside Family Laundry in the 1930s; the premises are now used by the Angle Snooker Club. The shop blind on the extreme left of the picture is for the Maypole Dairy Co. at No. 344, and the lady in the long dress is approaching a delivery cart belonging to W. H. Torrance, the bakers. Torrance, famous for their Kettledrum shortbread, had shops at 356 Morningside Road and 2 & 4 Comiston Road.

MORNINGSIDE, EDINBURGH.

Morningside Road Station, *c*.1911. Passengers reached the trains either through the small station building or by the wicket gate to its right. The station was opened to passenger traffic in 1884 on what was then known as the Edinburgh & Suburban South Side Junction Railway. Much of the early planning for the successful suburban line was undertaken by Thomas Bouch, designer of the ill-fated Tay Bridge, which collapsed with the loss of many lives on 28 December 1879. After the Tay Bridge disaster, Bouch was relieved of his commission on the suburban line and the final survey was done by George Trimble of Trimble & Peddie. On several occasions in the last decade proposals have been put forward to reopen the suburban line to passengers, but so far the idea has not come to fruition.

Morningside Road opposite Hermitage Terrace, looking south *c*.1909. This is still a busy section of the road with a variety of well patronised shops. Almost a century ago the shops were equally popular, but the description of some of the trades was quite different. In the photograph (from right to left) are: Alex Black, family grocer and wine merchant (No. 376); James Waldie & Sons, coal merchants order office (No. 380); Miss Morton, draper and silk mercer (No. 382, at the first blind); David L. Kerr, hatter, hosier, glover and shirtmaker (No. 384, second blind); M. & L. Johnston, drapers and haberdashers (No. 386); John Aitchison, wholesale stationer and printer (No. 390, third blind), at present occupied by Kay's Bookshop.

Newbattle Terrace, looking west towards Morningside Road, with Woodburn Avenue on the left. The line of the terrace is very ancient – at least early sixteenth century – when it was the main communication across the Burgh Muir between the roads to Linton and Liberton and also gave access to Grange House. Its early name was Grange Loan, then Cant's Loan after the Cant family who owned Grange House in the sixteenth and part of the seventeenth century. The western section, seen here in the photograph, was named Church Lane from about 1838 after Morningside Parish Church was built, and then took the name Newbattle Terrace in 1885.

Morningside Place, Edinburgh.

It is many years since a young, unaccompanied child was able to cross safely at the junction of Morningside Place and Morningside Road. When this photograph was taken in the first decade of the twentieth century there was not a single vehicle parked at the side of the road, and the only traffic was a slow-moving gentleman on a bicycle. The street was called Deuchar Place after William Deuchar of Wester Morningside when it was first laid out in 1823.

A delivery man, cyclists and pedestrians are the only signs of congestion in Morningside Park in the early twentieth century. When the street was first built in 1875 the section on the west side, near to the junction with Morningside Place, was known as Pentland Terrace. The name Morningside Park was not adopted until 1894. In the background is the tower and steeple of South Morningside Church (originally Braid Road Free Church), now Cluny Church Centre.

The scene is almost rural in Woodburn Terrace in 1905, looking north to Canaan Lane with Streatham House in the open ground beyond. The terrace was named in the 1870s after the Woodburn estate which lay to its east. Woodburn House, dating from 1812, was the home of George Ross who, for many years, took financial responsibility for the upkeep of the Old Schoolhouse in Morningside Road (see page 20). Prior to 1890 Egypt Farm occupied land and farm buildings just south of the Jordan Burn, believed to have been near the junction of present day Woodburn Terrace and Nile Grove.

Braid United Presbyterian Church was designed by the architect George Washington Browne to seat 750, and cost a total of £5,000. The foundation stone was laid on Saturday 9 October 1886 and the church was opened for public worship on 10 July 1887. Its congregation had previously worshipped under the first minister, the Revd Walter Brown, in a temporary iron church at the north end of Braid Road and Comiston Road on ground now occupied by the red sandstone tenement above the Hermitage Bar. Braid United Presbyterian Church became Braid United Free in 1900 and Braid Church in 1929. In 1990 it merged with the congregation of Morningside Parish Church to form Morningside Braid Parish Church. On the extreme left of the picture there is a sign for Morningside Family Laundry which occupied the adjacent site.

In 1914, when this photograph was taken, only the north side of Falcon Avenue had been built: it was not until 1938 that the south side was completed. The avenue takes its name from Falcon Hall, the elegant mansion which stood in grounds which stretched down to Canaan Lane. At the far end of the street, St Peter's Roman Catholic Church can just be seen beside the trees on the left. The church was designed by Robert S. Lorimer in 1906, and the adjacent St Peter's School was opened in 1910.

Postcards of railway stations have always been popular, even as long ago as 23 December 1917 when the sender of this one, Littlejohn of No. 6 Woodburn Terrace, wrote to an acquaintance in Birmingham referring to 'our Suburban Station', and adding that Rosyth Passenger Station was to be opened on 1 January. This view shows Morningside Road Station, looking east towards Blackford Station. The rear of the entrance from Morningside Road is clearly visible straddling the track, giving access to steps going down to both platforms. Projecting above the roofline of the station building on the westbound track are some ornamental stones from James MacDonald & Co., sculptors and vault builders in Belhaven Terrace. Their proximity to the railway tracks allowed them to announce in their advertising material that they could 'deliver at any railway station or shipping port in the United Kingdom or abroad'.

The Clock, Morningside Station, Edinburgh

3495.

This postcard was sent in October 1940, but the photograph could have been taken much earlier. It shows the main road junction at Morningside Station, looking south up Braid Road (left) and Comiston Road (right). Also visible are two of the area's main churches. Farthest left is St Matthew's Parish Church with the miniature steeple, and in the centre is South Morningside Church. St Matthew's was opened in 1890 and South Morningside in 1892. The two congregations united in 1974 to form Cluny Parish Church. The St Matthew's building was used for worship and the South Morningside building became Cluny Church Centre.

This photograph was probably taken during the last few years of Edinburgh's electric tramway system: the final service ran on 16 November 1956 from Braids via Bruntsfield, Tollcross and the Mound to Shrubhill depot. The picture shows car 173 on service 23 making the tight turn from Morningside Road into Belhaven Terrace, which was the terminus. Electric trams were fitted with controls at both ends and had reversible seats and trolleys as there was no system for turning the tram round at the terminus. To the left of the No. 23 tram the front of a No. 5 bus can just be seen at its terminus at the mouth of Cluny Avenue.

An Edinburgh Corporation Transport electric tram on service 15 en route for Braids, waiting for passengers to board at Morningside Station. The photograph was probably taken shortly before closure of the electric tram system in 1956. The premises on the corner of Belhaven Terrace and Morningside Road were occupied for many years by Baird the Bootmaker Ltd., who had several shops throughout Edinburgh. The site is now occupied by a branch of the Bank of Scotland.

An electric tram on service 23 photographed at the terminus in Belhaven Terrace on 24 May 1953. The complete absence of parked vehicles provides the opportunity to see some of the street furniture of the day. From left to right: an old-style telephone box; a small drinking fountain; a wire waste-paper basket fixed to the support pole for the overhead power cables; a police box; the original gateway to Morningside Cemetery; and a sign indicating 'Morningside Cemetery'.

This view of Morningside Station road junction dates from *c*.1900 – almost a decade before the clock was erected in the middle of the roadway. In the photograph its approximate position (subsequently moved) is occupied by a street light which has a sign on it reading 'Cars Stop', referring to the cable cars, one of which can be seen proceeding northwards. The junction is sufficiently traffic-free that the lady with the pram feels quite safe in stopping to pose for the photograph.

The same junction photographed from the opposite direction, with St Matthew's Parish Church and South Morningside Church on the left. The building facing the camera on the gushet site between Braid Road and Comiston Road was intended to be a hotel, planned at the time when the suburban line was being introduced. However, the idea never came to fruition. William Bell & Son's coach office can be seen to the left of the clock, which was presented to the people of Morningside in 1910 by three local town councillors, R. K. Inches, William Inman and William Torrance. Torrance's Tea Room is visible on the corner of Comiston Road and Belhaven Terrace. The small structure on the bridge parapet is occupied as a coal office and cab office.

When this photograph was taken around 1909, the area around Blackford Pond was remarkably clear of trees and vegetation compared to today. The boundary walls and paths and the line of the suburban railway in front of the houses are clearly visible. Blackford Hill was acquired by Edinburgh Corporation from the Trotters of Mortonhall in 1884, and was almost immediately made available to the public. The acquisition of such an important open space for the use of the general populace owes much to the determination of Lord Provost George Harrison, whose efforts are commemorated by the Harrison Arch in Observatory Road.

Blackford Hill, Pond, and Arthur's Seat from South Morningside.

"Blackford on whose uncultured breast,
Among the broom, and thorn, and whin,
A truant boy, I sought the nest,

Or listed, as I lay at rest,
While rose on breezes thin,
The murmur of the city crowd."—*Marmion.*

South Morningside from Blackford Hill

This interesting view from Blackford Hill of the Braid Estate in the course of development is, unfortunately, not dated. The line of Midmar Gardens runs from left to right across the picture, showing some houses almost completed and others in the course of construction. Midmar Gardens was planned around 1893, but only a handful of house-numbers appear in the *Edinburgh & Leith Post Office Directories* by 1902. There is no sign of Midmar Drive, which was laid out later (nearer to the camera) and occupied about 1910. The two steeples in the background – belonging to Cluny Church Centre and Cluny Parish Church – help with orientation.

Braid Road, looking north to Morningside Station, with Comiston Terrace on the left. Rather surprisingly, the postcard makes no reference to the most historical aspect of the picture. Roughly opposite the point where the four-storey tenements give way to the terraced villas there is a slightly lighter patch on the road surface. This is the site of the Hanging Stanes, and is now commemorated by a small plaque set into the pavement reading: THOMAS KELLY AND HENRY ORNEIL, THE LAST TWO HIGHWAYMEN IN SCOTLAND TO BE EXECUTED, WERE HANGED IN PUBLIC ON 25TH JANUARY 1815 FROM THE GALLOWS ERECTED ON THE TWO STANES STILL VISIBLE ON THE SPOT WHICH WAS WHERE THE ROBBERY TOOK PLACE. On 23 November 1814 Kelly and Orneil, alias O'Neil, attacked and robbed David Loch, a carter from Biggar, who was on his way on horseback to the city of Edinburgh. At their trial before the Lord Justice Clerk, the Hon. David Boyle, the two men were found guilty and sentenced to be hanged. In Boyle's words this punishment was to be carried out 'not at the ordinary place but on the spot where you robbed and assaulted David Loch, or as near as possible to that spot'. The hanging actually took place several hundred yards to the north of the scene of the crime.

Comiston Drive, looking west towards Craiglockhart Hill, c.1908. The drive was built around 1891 and took its name from Comiston Road, even although it was not built on the Comiston estate which lies half a mile to the south-east.

South Morningside School in Comiston Road was designed by the architect Robert Wilson in 1891, and was opened to pupils on 5 September 1892 under the control of St Cuthbert's and Dean School Board. Within the first few days the enrolment reached 572, made up of pupils from the Old Schoolhouse, Gorgie School, James Gillespie's and numerous small private schools in the district. The school was officially opened on 3 October 1892 by Professor Masson of Edinburgh University, who contrasted the new accommodation with the elementary schools of 60 years previously. Among those present were Hew Morrison, chairman of the School Board, and Andrew Carnegie, whose business interests in the iron and steel industries of America later financed his vast philanthropic programme in his native Scotland. When the school celebrated its centenary in 1992 its history was written by a group of parents and staff under the title *South Morningside School: A Centenary History, 1892–1992*.

Braidburn Terrace.

The south side of Braidburn Terrace was designed in 1906 by W. H. A. Ross and built by David Adamson & Son of Morningside. At the extreme right-hand edge of the photograph is the detached house Strathairly, built in 1903 for the artist John Michael Brown. At one time Braidburn Terrace was known as Greenbank Road, taking its name from the narrow track which led from Braid Road to Greenbank Farm. The photograph is taken from Braid Road looking across what are now the tennis courts of Mortonhall Tennis Club to the rear of the houses on the south side of the terrace.

Braidburn Dairy (right) lay to the east of Braid Road between the garden ground of the house known as Strathairly and land occupied firstly by a curling pond and then by Mortonhall Tennis Club. In 1891 the dairyman was William Mitchell, who lived there with his wife and family and two servants. Braid Road was the turnpike road from Morningside to West Linton and Biggar. In an effort to avoid the worst of the bad bends and steep gradient, the road was realigned to the west in 1830 along what is now Comiston Road, Pentland Terrace and Buckstone Terrace.

This was the idyllic setting of Mortonhall Curling Pond House, situated on the low ground below Braidburn Terrace that is now occupied by the clubhouse of Mortonhall Tennis Club. The date of construction and original purpose of the house is not known, but it was used by the curling club from around 1890 to 1914. Tennis was played on the site from about 1914, although the records of Mortonhall Tennis Club do not date back before 1926. For many years the lower storey of the building was used by the tennis club as a clubhouse, but the old building was demolished in 1957 when it was replaced by a more appropriate structure.

This photograph was taken from the position of present-day Fly Walk, near Greenbank Crescent, looking east across what is now Braidburn Valley Public Park to the Braid Hills Hotel and the houses of Pentland Terrace. When the photograph was taken *c*.1910, this land still formed part of Greenbank Farm. The farmhouse and steadings were on the corner of present-day Greenbank Loan and Gardens, and before the turnpike road was realigned in 1830 (to form Comiston Road and Pentland Terrace) the lands of Greenbank stretched as far as Braid Road to include the area now known as Riselaw.

The Braid Hills Hotel was built in the 1890s on a commanding site between Braid Road and Pentland Terrace, which at that time was in open countryside. Two of its early attractions were the proximity of the golf courses on the Braid Hills and the reliability of public transport in the form of cable cars, which ran every three minutes up until 11.30 p.m. Visitors to the hotel had the use of a spacious coffee room, drawing room, billiard room, reading room and smoking room, and there were excursions by carriage to Habbie's Howe, the Forth Bridge and Swanston. Over the years the hotel has been extended on several occasions, but the two original stained-glass windows depicting golf scenes have been retained, one of which includes the professional, James Braid, who first won the Open in 1901 at Muirfield.

BRAID HILLS HOTEL, EDINBURGH.

43

An open-topped cable car at the Braids terminus in Pentland Terrace with the crossover line clearly visible on the road. Cars were hauled along by a cable which ran below the level of the road surface in a slot between the rails. When the cable broke (as it frequently did) all the cars on that section were immobilised until the repair was attended to. The substantial timber shelter to the left was for the convenience of passengers waiting for a car and was also used by the car driver and conductor. The estate wall which forms a gateway beside the shelter was demolished many years ago and replaced with high metal railings.

The old thatched cottage at Lothianburn was a well-known landmark on the right-hand side of the road to Biggar near the right of way to Swanston village. When Lothianburn Golf Club was founded in 1893 only a very modest clubhouse was erected. However, in 1896 the club had the idea of using the thatched cottage as the basis of a new clubhouse. The plan was to use the existing floor space as the greenkeeper's house and build a second storey for the clubrooms. However, the plan was abandoned in favour of retaining the cottage as the greenkeeper's house only, and building a new (and again fairly basic) clubhouse, which was opened on 3 October 1896. In 1909 a much more substantial clubhouse was built on the site by James Miller of Morningside and opened by Major Trotter on 24 September 1910. This is the building to the left of the thatched cottage.

At the foot of the Pentlands, Swanston
" Be it granted to me to behold you again in dying,
Hills of home! and to hear again the call

(Copyright))   James Patrick
Hear about the graves of the martyrs, the peewees crying
And hear no more at all "—Songs of Travel, R.L.S.

The fields in the foreground of this picture were ploughed and furrowed for many generations before the ground was acquired for the construction of the Edinburgh City Bypass, first planned in the 1930s. To the left is the T wood on the lower slopes of Caerketton Hill, which was laid out in 1766 by Henry Trotter of Mortonhall. Although seen as T-shaped from Edinburgh, it is actually in the form of a Maltese cross, which rather detracts from the notion that the wood was planted by the Trotter family to assert dominion over their land after the family's unsuccessful legal dispute with the City of Edinburgh over water rights at Swanston. The old village of Swanston nestles in the trees to the right-hand side of the picture.

Swanston Cottage was constructed in 1761 as a small single-storey thatched building used by the City of Edinburgh in connection with the town's water supply from springs at Swanston. Power to use the water was given by an Act of Parliament in 1758. The cottage was greatly enlarged around 1835 when the magistrates added a second storey and replaced the thatch with slate. Bow windows were also built out at the front and a single-storey addition was constructed to the east. By far its most interesting era, however, began in 1867 when Thomas Stevenson, father of Robert Louis Stevenson, took the tenancy of the house as a summer retreat. Swanston Cottage became the romantic setting and inspiration for many of Stevenson's poems and novels, particularly *St Ives*.

Swanston Farmhouse lies immediately adjacent to the old village of Swanston. The L-plan building, dating from the early eighteenth century, has not always been maintained to the standards expected of a category B listed building. After it ceased to be used as a farmhouse in 1959 it provided accommodation for casual labourers at the harvest and potato-lifting seasons. During this period its condition deteriorated greatly, despite protests by various conservation bodies. Following a serious fire in 1984 the property was acquired by a firm of builders who renovated the entire property and converted it into three distinctive houses around a U-shaped courtyard. In this picture Swanston farm steadings are out of view to the right of the horses and carts.

Swanston village is one of the most picturesque locations in present-day Edinburgh, with whitewashed cottages, thatched roofs and a total absence of commercialisation. At the end of the Second World War the scene was very different. The eighteenth-century cottages still had earth floors, and no electricity or piped water. This was all the more ironic considering that electricity power lines hung from pylons a few hundred yards away, and Swanston was one of the main sources of Edinburgh's early water supply. Electricity was installed in the village in 1949 but it was not until 1956 that an ambitious scheme, estimated to cost £17,000, was put forward by the City Architect for the conversion of nine old cottages into seven renovated dwellings. Their thatched roofs would be retained, but modern fittings installed. By 1960 the eventual cost of renovation was nearer to £26,000. Edinburgh Corporation then invited tenders from more than 90 eager applicants to rent one of the completed houses. In this early twentieth century photograph, stooks of corn, ripening in the sun, stand in the field on the higher ground to the south of the village.